MW01689390

is the Church?

4-week course to help senior highers explore the mission of the church as God's agent in a needy world

by Deena Borchers

Group®
Loveland, Colorado

What Is the Church?
Copyright © 1992 Group Publishing, Inc.

First Printing

All rights reserved. No part of this book may be reproduced in any manner whatsoever without written permission from the publisher, except where noted on handouts and in the case of brief quotations embodied in critical articles and reviews. For information write Permissions, Group Books, Box 481, Loveland, CO 80539.

Credits
Edited by Lois Keffer, Steve Parolini and Paul Woods
Cover designed by Jill Nordbye and DeWain Stoll
Interior designed by Judy Bienick and Jan Aufdemberge
Illustrations by Raymond Medici
Cover photo by Brenda Rundback

ISBN 1-55945-222-6
Printed in the United States of America

CONTENTS

INTRODUCTION

WHAT IS THE CHURCH?

> *Hilarion asked, "Are you a Christian?" And I answered, "I am a Christian." And when my father persisted in his attempts to dissuade me, Hilarion ordered him thrown out, and he was beaten with a rod . . . Then the sentence was passed; all of us were condemned to the beasts . . .(A Lost Tradition: Women Writers of the Early Church,* University Press of America*)*

These words come from the diary of Perpetua, a wealthy young woman of the third century who had just given birth to a child and had everything to live for. In Perpetua's day it was illegal to practice Christianity. She chose to die a martyr rather than renounce her faith.

For many teenagers, stories of early Christians seem like fairy tales about super heroes of long ago. Kids in your group need to see that early Christians had many of the same fears, shortcomings and doubts they do. Early Christians were common people who, by the power of the Holy Spirit, did uncommon things.

Early Christians faced and conquered overwhelming challenges. Today's teenagers face overwhelming challenges of their own. Your kids will be encouraged by identifying with their first-century brothers and sisters in Christ and seeing how they endured persecution with a courageous witness and uncompromising faith.

Christianity isn't meant for the fainthearted or complacent. The church was instituted by Christ to "preach good news to the poor . . . proclaim freedom for the prisoners . . . to release the oppressed, to proclaim the year of the Lord's favor" (from Luke 4:18). Teenagers are idealistic: They love a cause. Your group will be excited to see the church as the radical body it should be.

The Holy Spirit continues to inspire people today to carry out God's mission in new and creative ways. Teenagers' minds are wide open to God's leading— their insights are invaluable to both the present and the future of the church. So explore these four lessons together and help your teenagers each discover their role in Christ's church— then watch and listen as they make it happen.

COURSE OBJECTIVES

By the end of this course, your students will:

- understand the role of the Holy Spirit in directing and empowering Christ's followers;
- learn how to deal with persecution;
- see the importance of taking a bold stand for Christ through words and actions; and
- discover how to get personally involved in the mission of the church.

HOW TO USE THIS COURSE

ACTIVE LEARNING

Think back on an important lesson you've learned in life. Did you learn it from reading about it? from hearing about it? from something you experienced? Chances are, the most important lessons you've learned came from something you've experienced. That's what active learning is— learning by doing. And active learning is a key element in Group's Active Bible Curriculum™.

Active learning leads students in doing things that help them understand important principles, messages and ideas. It's a discovery process that helps kids internalize what they learn.

Each lesson section in Group's Active Bible Curriculum plays an important part in active learning:

The **Opener** involves kids in the topic in fun and unusual ways.

The **Action and Reflection** includes an experience designed to evoke specific feelings in the students. This section also processes those feelings through "How did you feel?" questions and applies the message to situations kids face.

The **Bible Application** actively connects the topic with the Bible. It helps kids see how the Bible is relevant to the situations they face.

The **Commitment** helps students internalize the Bible's message and commit to making changes in their lives.

The **Closing** funnels the lesson's message into a time of creative reflection and prayer.

When you put all the sections together, you get a lesson that's fun to teach. And kids get messages they'll remember.

BEFORE THE 4-WEEK SESSION

- Read the Introduction, the Course Objectives and This Course at a Glance.
- Decide how you'll publicize the course using the clip art on the Publicity Page (p. 9). Prepare fliers, newsletter articles and posters as needed.
- Look at the Bonus Ideas (p. 43) and decide which ones you'll use.

BEFORE EACH LESSON

- Read the opening statements, Objectives and Bible Basis for the lesson. The Bible Basis shows how specific passages relate to senior highers today.
- Choose which Opener and Closing options to use. Each is appropriate for a different kind of group.
- Gather necessary supplies from This Lesson at a Glance.
- Read each section of the lesson. Adjust where necessary for your class size and meeting room.

HELPFUL HINTS

- The approximate minutes listed give you an idea of how long each activity will take. Each lesson is designed to take 35 to 60 minutes. Shorten or lengthen activities as needed to fit your group.
- If you see you're going to have extra time, do an activity or two from the "If You Still Have Time . . ." box or from the Bonus Ideas (p. 43).
- Dive into the activities with the kids. Don't be a spectator. The lesson will be more successful and rewarding to both you and your students.
- Though some kids may at first think certain activities are "silly," they'll enjoy them, and they'll remember the messages from these activities long after the lesson is over. As one Active Bible Curriculum user has said, "I can ask the kids questions about a lesson I did three weeks ago, and they actually remember what I taught!" And that's the whole idea of teaching . . . isn't it?

Have fun with the activities you lead. Remember, it is Jesus who encourages us to become "like little children." Besides, how often do your kids get *permission* to express their childlike qualities?

> - The answers given after discussion questions are responses your students *might* give. They aren't the only answers or the "right" answers. If needed, use them to spark discussion. Kids won't always say what you wish they'd say. That's why some of the responses given are negative or controversial. If someone responds negatively, don't be shocked. Accept the person and use the opportunity to explore other angles of the issue.

THIS COURSE AT A GLANCE

Before you dive into the lessons, familiarize yourself with each lesson aim. Then read the scripture passages.

- Study them as a background to the lessons.
- Use them as a basis for your personal devotions.
- Think about how they relate to kids' circumstances today.

LESSON 1: THE BIRTHDAY OF THE CHURCH

Lesson Aim: To help senior highers understand the role of the Holy Spirit in directing and empowering Christ's followers.

Bible Basis: Joel 2:28-32 and Acts 2:1-13.

LESSON 2: STAND STRONG

Lesson Aim: To help senior highers understand that the Holy Spirit empowers Christians to live out their faith in the face of opposition.

Bible Basis: Acts 4:1-21; Acts 12:1-16; and Romans 8:31-39.

LESSON 3: TAKING THE CHURCH ON THE ROAD

Lesson Aim: To help senior highers discover the importance of telling others about their faith.

Bible Basis: Acts 8:26-40 and Ephesians 4:11-13.

LESSON 4: ON A MISSION

Lesson Aim: To help senior highers discover the mission God gave the church and how they can help fulfill it.

Bible Basis: Acts 1:6-8; Acts 10:34-43; and Acts 14:21-23.

PUBLICITY PAGE

Grab your senior highers' attention! Photocopy this page and then cut and paste the clip art of your choice in your church bulletin or newsletter to advertise this course on the early church. Or photocopy and use the ready-made flier as a bulletin insert.

Permission to photocopy clip art is granted for local church use.

Splash the clip art on posters, fliers or even postcards! Just add the vital details: the date and time the course begins, and where you'll meet.

It's that simple.

What is the Church?

What is the Church?

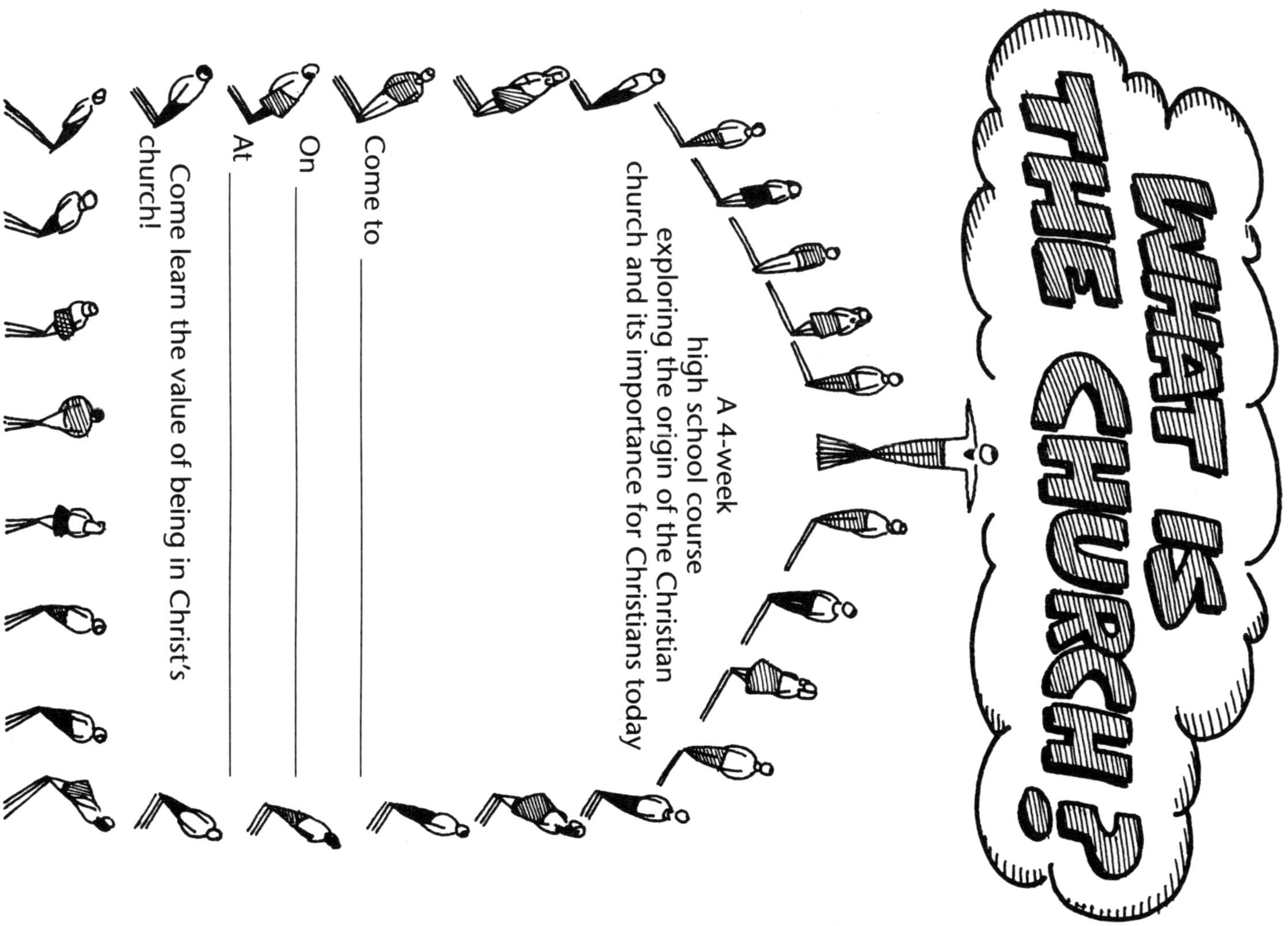

THE BIRTHDAY OF THE CHURCH

LESSON 1

A birth is always an exciting event, and the birth of the church is no exception. On the day of Pentecost, the Holy Spirit paid an extraordinary visit to a small group of Christians, empowering and galvanizing them into a dynamic, world-changing force. Kids need to know that the Holy Spirit is still at work in the church today. This lesson will help your kids catch the excitement of opening themselves to God's Holy Spirit and being part of God's special force in a needy world.

LESSON AIM

To help senior highers understand the role of the Holy Spirit in directing and empowering Christ's followers.

OBJECTIVES

Students will:

- **discover how the Holy Spirit directs and empowers the church;**
- **realize the importance of making God's Word understandable to all people;**
- **discover ways to allow the Holy Spirit to work in their lives; and**
- **make commitments to open themselves to the power and leading of the Holy Spirit.**

BIBLE BASIS

JOEL 2:28-32
ACTS 2:1-13

Look up the following scriptures. Then read the background paragraphs to see how the passages relate to your senior highers.

Joel 2:28-32 is the prophecy we see fulfilled in Acts 2:1-13 on the day of Pentecost. Joel prophesies that God's spirit will be poured out on "all people," not just a select few prophets or leaders. From Pentecost forward, God's people are no longer only those born of Jewish parentage, but those "who call on the name of the Lord."

Acts 2:1-13 tells the story of the birth of the church. Jews from many countries were gathered in Jerusalem for the feast of Pentecost, a Jewish thanksgiving or harvest feast. With great power and spectacle, the Holy Spirit broke down language barriers and enabled the disciples to spread the good news to people who would not otherwise understand. As those people went back to their homes, they took with them the exciting news of eternal life through faith in Jesus Christ. The church was off and running!

The Holy Spirit came to obedient, praying people who dedicated themselves as a body to seeking and praying for God's will. When the church today meets these conditions, the Holy Spirit still comes in power, enabling Christians to carry out God's work in the world.

THIS LESSON AT A GLANCE

Section	Minutes	What Students Will Do	Supplies
Opener (Option 1)	5 to 10	**Surprise Me**—Let inflated balloons go and compare the excitement and their unpredictable paths with being led by the Holy Spirit.	Balloons
(Option 2)		**Happy Birthday**—Celebrate the birthday of the church.	Cake or cupcakes, trick candles, matches
Action and Reflection	10 to 15	**Say What?**—Experience how it feels not to be able to understand an important message.	"The Sky Is Falling" handouts (p. 18)
Bible Application	10 to 15	**The Church in the News**—Create a news broadcast based on the events in Joel 2 and Acts 2.	Pencils, paper, Bibles, assignment slips
Commitment	5 to 10	**Jammed!**—Use loud music to disrupt communication.	Two boomboxes, Bibles
Closing (Option 1)	5 to 10	**Power to Spare**—Pray for power to witness.	Power cord
(Option 2)		**Shine On**—Use candles that won't go out while praying for God's help in sharing that gospel.	Trick candles, matches, cup of water

The Lesson

OPENER
(5 to 10 minutes)

☐ OPTION 1: SURPRISE ME

Distribute balloons. Have kids each blow up a balloon and hold the end without tying it. When all the balloons are blown up, say: **We're all going to let our balloons go on the count of three. Ready? One . . . two . . . three!**

Have kids each retrieve their balloon. Then ask:

● **How is letting a balloon go like letting the Holy Spirit work in your life?** (You can't really tell what direction it will go or where it will end up; it's unpredictable and exciting.)

Hold up a balloon and ask:

● **How do we as Christians compare to this uninflated balloon?** (We need to be filled by God's power; we can't fill ourselves.)

Blow up a balloon and hold the end. Hold it up next to the limp, uninflated balloon. Say: **Christians who open themselves to the Holy Spirit are ready to go places and do things for God. Life is an adventure.** Have kids blow up their balloons and hold the ends. **When a whole group of Christians with the Holy Spirit living in them gets together, life is doubly exciting. Living with God's power can absolutely blow you away!** Have kids release their balloons. **The book of Acts tells us how God unleashed his power on a group of sincere believers. The marvelous events of that day changed the course of history and still have a profound effect on our lives today. Let's get in on the action and see what happened.**

☐ OPTION 2: HAPPY BIRTHDAY

Bring out a birthday cake or cupcakes topped with trick candles. Light the candles and say: **It's always great to start things off with food. But before anyone can eat, you have to guess whose birthday we're celebrating. Any guesses?** Listen to kids' guesses.

If no one guesses correctly, say: **I'll give you a few clues.**

● **This birth was marked by supernatural events.**

● **There was fire, but not from birthday candles.**

● **There was the sound of wind, but it was no ordinary wind.**

● **This isn't the birth of a person.**

If kids haven't guessed by now, explain that you're talking about the birth of the church at Pentecost. Tell kids you've made them look at this food long enough—it's time to blow out the candles and eat. Have a volunteer try to blow out the candles. The trick candles will keep popping out with new flames.

Ask:

● **How do these candles that refuse to go out remind you of the early Christians?** (Despite persecution and efforts to stamp out Christianity, they refused to give up; they persistently shared their faith and the church grew.)

Say: **Of course, the early Christians didn't accomplish all this on their own. They were guided and empowered by the Holy Spirit. Today we're going to take a look at what happened on the day of Pentecost and see how those events still affect our lives today.**

Pass out pieces of birthday cake or cupcakes.

ACTION AND REFLECTION

(10 to 15 minutes)

SAY WHAT?

Cut apart slips from "The Sky Is Falling!" handout (p. 18) and fold them. Give kids each one slip.

Say: **Don't look at your slips until I tell you to. Then read what it says and follow the directions immediately. Ready? Look now!**

Most of the kids will dive under the table. Those who received instructions in French or Japanese will probably just stand there looking bewildered. Others may urge them to get under the table. If no one tells them what to do, say: **Don't you understand this? It says: "The sky is falling! Get under the table." Now!**

After everyone has crawled under the table, squat down and say: **Good job! If the story of Chicken Little ever comes true, you guys and girls have it made. Okay—it's all clear. You can come out now.**

Have kids return to their seats. Then ask those who received instructions in French or Japanese:

● **How did you feel being the only ones who didn't know what to do?** (Weird; left out; vulnerable.)

● **How did you feel toward the person who helped you understand what you needed to do to be safe?** (Grateful.)

● **How is this experience like what happened to the foreigners in Jerusalem at Pentecost?** (They saw something exciting happening but not everyone understood. Then they were able to understand and respond because they each heard the disciples in their own language.)

Say: **God's timing for the birth of the church was perfect. Jerusalem was filled with visitors who had come to attend the Feast of Harvest. By God's miraculous power, these people were able to hear the disciples in their own languages. No one was left out! Let's find out more about what happened on this remarkable birthday.**

THE CHURCH IN THE NEWS

BIBLE APPLICATION
(10 to 15 minutes)

Have a volunteer read Acts 2:1-13 aloud.

Say: **If something like this happened today, it would be a major media event. Since the main source of news of that time was word of mouth, we're going to travel back in time and supply the missing elements. You're about to become reporters, editors and interviewees for the Jerusalem Nightly News.**

Have kids form three groups. Give groups each a pencil and a sheet of paper and enough Bibles for every two or three students. Write the following assignments and scripture passages on slips of paper and give one to each group: Supernatural Events Reported (Acts 2:1-8); Eyewitness Interviews (Acts 2:5-13); Prophecy Fulfilled? (Joel 2:28-32).

Say: **Your job is to prepare a report on the topic you've been given for the Jerusalem Nightly News. You can use any format for your news report—go with an anchor-person, co-anchors, interviews, commentaries—whatever! Air time is in five minutes. Go to it!**

As kids are working in their groups, set up a table and chairs for the news reports. After five minutes call everyone together and have groups present their reports. Applaud each group's efforts.

Then ask:

- **How did it feel to imagine being part of the events at Pentecost?** (It was awesome; it was hard to imagine actually experiencing these things.)
- **Why do you think God chose to send his spirit and demonstrate his power in the ways he did?** (God sent the Holy Spirit to the believers who were praying so they would have power and boldness to preach; God gave the gift of speaking and understanding other languages so that all of the people gathered could understand and respond to the Gospel.)
- **Why do you think we refer to Pentecost as the birth of the church?** (That's when the Spirit came upon Jesus' followers and sent them out into the world as God's messengers.)

Say: **At Pentecost, the Holy Spirit took a group of confused, frightened Christians and molded them into a dynamic force that changed the world. The Holy Spirit is still in the business of empowering and directing Christians today. Our next activity will give us some clues about how we can allow the Holy Spirit to work in our lives.**

JAMMED!

COMMITMENT
(5 to 10 minutes)

Set up two boomboxes on opposite sides of the room. Play lively music on one boombox at medium volume.

Say: **I'm going to read you something. Please listen carefully and be ready to answer questions.**

Read Acts 2:38-47 in a normal speaking voice. As you read, turn on the second boombox with loud music. Then walk over to the first boombox and turn up the volume to the point that you can barely be heard as you continue to read in a normal voice.

After you've finished reading the scripture passage, turn off both boomboxes. Ask kids two or three questions about what you read, such as:

- **Who did Peter say the promise was for?**
- **What did the believers do with their possessions?**
- **Where did they meet together?**

Kids will probably be unable to answer because they couldn't hear you over the noise of the boomboxes.

Ask:

- **How did you feel trying to hear me through all that noise?** (Frustrated; confused.)
- **How is that like trying to tune in to the Holy Spirit through all the busyness of our lives?** (We need to receive the Holy Spirit's power and guidance, but we get too busy to listen.)
- **How can we allow the Holy Spirit to work in our lives?** (We can "turn off" some things that fill our time, such as television or long telephone conversations.)

Note: This would be an excellent time to bring in your pastor or other leader from your congregation to discuss with kids your denomination's teaching about the role of the Holy Spirit in the life of a Christian.

Say: **It's important to remember that the Holy Spirit came to people who were praying, waiting and listening. Even if we do have a daily prayer time, we may not always take time to wait and listen for the Holy Spirit's guidance. Find a partner right now and tell that person how and when you're going to invite the Holy Spirit to speak to you this week.**

Allow one or two minutes for partners to talk with each other. Then bring everyone together for closing activities.

Table Talk

The Table Talk activity in this course helps senior highers talk with their parents about how the Holy Spirit activates and empowers individual Christians and the church as a whole.

If you choose to use the Table Talk activity, this is a good time to show students the "Table Talk" handout (p. 19). Ask them to spend time with their parents completing it.

Before kids leave, give them each the "Table Talk" handout to take home, or tell them you'll be sending it to their parents. Tell kids to be prepared to report on their experiences with the handout next week.

Or use the Table Talk idea found in the Bonus Ideas (p. 43) for a meeting based on the handout.

CLOSING

(5 to 10 minutes)

☐ OPTION 1: POWER TO SPARE

Lay a power cord on the floor in a circle. Have kids stand in a circle around the cord.

Have kids pick up and hold the power cord.

Ask:

- **How is this cord like the Holy Spirit?** (It empowers things like the Holy Spirit empowers us.)

Close with a prayer similar to this one: **Thank you, Lord, for making the Holy Spirit's power available to us. Help us take time to plug in to that power by listening to the Holy Spirit as we pray. We ask you to energize us and send us out into the world as your witnesses. In Jesus' name. Amen.**

☐ OPTION 2: SHINE ON

Give kids each a trick candle. Light the candle you're holding.

Ask:

- **As we go out into the world as God's representatives this week, how will we be like this candle?** (We'll represent Jesus who offers the light of love in place of sin and despair; we'll be empowered by the Holy Spirit who cannot be extinguished.)

Pass the flame from your candle around the circle. When all the candles have been lit, say: **Just as many candles bring more light to a dark place than one single flame, our combined witness as a church can have a greater impact than any one of us alone.**

Close with a brief prayer thanking God for your church and the church around the world. Ask God's help and blessing in bringing the light of the gospel to those who have never heard.

Have students extinguish their candles in a cup of water.

If You Still Have Time . . .

Church Affirmations—Have kids discuss the kind of impact your church has in your community through organized programs or the efforts of individuals and groups within the church. Invite kids to share stories about how the church has made a difference in people's lives, including their own.

That Was Then, This Is Now—Form two groups. Have one group tell why it would be neat to travel back in time and be part of the first century church. Have the other group tell why they'd rather be part of the church today.

THE SKY *Is* FALLING!

PHOTOCOPY THIS HANDOUT AND CUT APART THE STRIPS. MAKE ENOUGH PHOTOCOPIES SO THAT EACH STUDENT CAN RECEIVE A SET OF INSTRUCTIONS.

The sky is falling! Get under the table.

The sky is falling! Get under the table.

The sky is falling! Get under the table.

The sky is falling! Get under the table.

Le ciel tombe! Mettez-vous sous la table.

Le ciel tombe! Mettez-vous sous la table.

The sky is falling! Get under the table.

The sky is falling! Get under the table.

The sky is falling! Get under the table.

The sky is falling! Get under the table.

そら が おちいる テーブル の した に いき たさい.

そら が おちいる テーブル の した に いき たさい.

Permission to photocopy this handout granted for local church use. Copyright © Group Publishing, Inc., Box 481, Loveland, CO 80539.

Table Talk

To the Parent: We're involved in a high school course at church called *What Is the Church?* Students are exploring the role of the church in the world and how the Holy Spirit empowers and directs Christians to accomplish God's purposes. We'd like you and your teenager to spend some time discussing this important topic. Use this "Table Talk" page to help you do that.

Parent and senior higher

Complete the following sentences:

- One time the church really made a difference in my life was . . .
- Something that makes me glad to be a part of our church is . . .
- I think one real strength of our church is . . .
- One thing I'd like to see changed about our church is . . .
- I think we could work toward that change by . . .

Discuss:

- What makes a church dynamic and effective in its community.
- Why the church always seems to grow and thrive in the face of persecution.
- What the mission of the church should be both locally and globally.
- What gifts you as individuals and as a family bring to your congregation and how they fit into the church's mission.

Talk together about how you might react if your government suddenly made Christianity a crime. Would you stand up for your beliefs and risk jail or even death? Or would you keep silent and not tell others about your faith?

Read Acts 2:42-47 together. Discuss how your church compares to this New Testament model. Decide on one definite step you can take as a family to promote this kind of fellowship in your church.

What is the Church?

Permission to photocopy this handout granted for local church use. Copyright © Group Publishing, Inc., Box 481, Loveland, CO 80539.

LESSON 2

STAND STRONG

God's faithful followers have never been exempt from hardship. Over the centuries Christians have endured concerted efforts by people outside (and inside) the church to stamp out their faith. But the amazing thing about the church is that the more people try to stamp it out, the more it grows!

Though today's teenagers may not face death or imprisonment, they're not exempt from being persecuted for their faith. This lesson will help kids see that they can stand strong and grow in their faith during times of hardship, just as the early Christians did.

LESSON AIM

To help senior highers understand that the Holy Spirit empowers Christians to live out their faith in the face of opposition.

OBJECTIVES

Students will:
- **understand the cost of discipleship both in the early church and today;**
- **see how God comforts Christians in times of hardship and persecution;**
- **learn how to respond to persecution; and**
- **grow in their commitment to spreading the gospel.**

BIBLE BASIS

ACTS 4:1-21
ACTS 12:1-16
ROMANS 8:31-39

Look up the following scriptures. Then read the background paragraphs to see how the passages relate to your senior highers.

In **Acts 4:1-21** we read of Peter's courageous response when the members of the Sanhedrin ordered him not to speak or teach in the name of Jesus.

This incident followed the healing of the lame man at the temple gate. Peter answered a well-known beggar's request for alms with much more than the beggar expected. The astonished crowd gathered around to find out by what power Peter had accomplished this miracle. Peter told them that the lame man was made strong "by faith in the name of Jesus."

The temple leaders tried to put a stop to Peter's witness with jail and threats. Peter responded boldly, saying that he would obey God rather than men. Kids today may well face ridicule for honoring Jesus' name in front of their peers. But God can help them speak boldly for Christ as Peter did.

In **Acts 12:1-16**, we read of the persecution of Christians under King Herod. James the son of Zebedee had been put to death by Herod. When James' execution brought cheers from the Jewish leaders, Herod decided to go for one more head—Peter's. An angel miraculously released Peter from his chains. Peter joined the Christians who had been in an all-night prayer meeting for his safety. Together they rejoiced in God's deliverance.

Christian teenagers may sometimes feel helpless and overwhelmed in a godless environment. But God is—and always has been—in the business of answering prayer, sometimes with miraculous power.

Romans 8:31-39 is the victory cry of an apostle who would eventually make the supreme sacrifice for his faith. In this passage Paul assures Christians that God's love literally conquers all.

It's pretty easy for teenagers to feel overwhelmed by life. Many of the decisions they make as Christians are counter-cultural, and open them to criticism and ridicule. At times your kids may feel like giving up. Paul's words encourage them to hang in there and believe that in the end they will be "more than conquerors."

THIS LESSON AT A GLANCE

Section	Minutes	What Students Will Do	Supplies
Opener (Option 1)	5 to 10	**Cola Wars**—Receive special treatment or be penalized based on their choice of colas.	Paper, marker, masking tape
(Option 2)		**Get the Red Out**—Experience discrimination based on wearing the color red.	Doughnuts or other treats, masking tape
Action and Reflection	10 to 15	**Diego's Dilemma**—Perform a skit about persecution of Christians.	"Diego's Dilemma" hand-outs (p. 27)
Bible Application	15 to 20	**To Speak or Not to Speak?**—Discover biblical principles for responding to persecution.	Pencils, paper, Bibles, newsprint and marker or chalkboard and chalk
Commitment	5 to 10	**Comfort Zone**—Assure others of God's help in their lives.	1-foot lengths of ribbon
Closing (Option 1)	up to 5	**Circle Prayer**—Pray for kids facing persecution.	
(Option 2)		**Unbreakable Bond**—Tie an unbreakable human knot.	

The Lesson

OPENER
(5 to 10 minutes)

☐ OPTION 1: COLA WARS

Hang a sign that says "Coke" on one side of the room. On the other side of the room hang a sign that says "Pepsi."

As kids come in, have them sit down by the sign that shows their preferred soft drink. If kids don't like either cola, ask them to choose the cola they dislike the least and sit by that sign. If all kids go the the Pepsi side, assign a few kids to stand on the Coke side.

Say to all the Coke drinkers: **I have bad news. This is a Pepsi day. I'm afraid you guys and girls are going to have to be penalized for your choice of soft drinks. If you just sit quietly, things won't be too bad for you.**

Have the Pepsi drinkers help you put a piece of tape over the mouths of all the Coke drinkers. Emphasize the need for gentleness in this activity, and be sure to use tape that will come off easily.

Now, with the Coke drinkers' mouths taped shut, encourage the Pepsi drinkers to talk about how much better Pepsi is than Coke. After a minute or two, call a halt to the conversation and allow the Coke drinkers to remove their tape.

Ask:

- **How did you feel being treated like this just because your choice was different from someone else's? Explain.** (Angry because I was being treated unfairly; humiliated because they put tape over my mouth and I couldn't defend my choice.)
- **How is this like what sometimes happens because you choose to be a follower of Christ?** (Sometimes people treat you unfairly; they don't give you a chance to speak up for what you believe.)
- **What do people do to keep you from talking about your beliefs?** (They make fun of you; they refuse to listen; they make you feel stupid for believing what you do.)

Say: **When you face hard times because of your faith, you're in good company. Since the days of the early church, Christians have been persecuted in one way or another. You may not have to face hungry lions, but nobody can say that taking ridicule from your peers is easy. Today we're going to look at how early Christians reacted to persecution and discover how God helps us deal with whatever comes our way.**

☐ OPTION 2: GET THE RED OUT

Bring treats, such as doughnuts or cookies. Ask all the kids who have anything red on to go to one corner of the room. (If no one is wearing red, choose another color some kids are wearing.) Mark off a small space with masking tape and tell the kids wearing red to squeeze into the space and remain there until you say they can leave. Serve the treats to the remaining kids. As you eat, talk about how obnoxious the color red is.

When the kids have finished eating, tell the kids wearing red they can join you and have some of the treats.

Ask:

- **How did you feel being excluded from sharing the food on the basis of what you're wearing?** (Angry; unwanted.)
- **How is this like what sometimes happens to kids who take a stand for Christ?** (Other kids let you know they don't want you around; they plan activities they know you won't participate in.)
- **What have other kids done to make you feel excluded or out of place because you are a Christian?** (Talked about wild parties they've attended; used gross language to get me to leave; talked about how weird Christianity is.)

Say: **Being excluded is hard. It's especially hard being excluded for doing what's right. Exclusion is one form of persecution almost every Christian experiences from time to time. Today we're going to look at how to handle that persecution and what God does to help us through it.**

Table Talk Follow-Up

If you sent the "Table Talk" handout (p. 19) to parents last week, discuss students' reactions to the activity. Ask volunteers to share what they learned from the discussion with their parents.

ACTION AND REFLECTION

(10 to 15 minutes)

DIEGO'S DILEMMA

Choose two volunteers to read the parts of the father and teenager. Give them each a "Diego's Dilemma" handout (p. 27) and ask them to stand facing each other in the center of the room. Have the rest of the class form two teams. Have one team stand behind each character and cheer him on with comments such as, "That's right," and "Yeah—you're on a roll." Each team will also harrass the other character with comments such as, "Come on—get real," and "No way!"

Introduce the drama, saying: **There are places in the world today where Christians face life-threatening persecution for putting their faith into action. This imaginary drama is set in El Salvador at the house of a government official, Señor Gonzales, who is a Christian. Señor Gonzales and his son Diego are discussing appropriate ways to live out their faith in Christ in response to the difficult situation in their country.**

Have the two volunteers each read their part while the two teams harrass them.

After the drama, have kids applaud the efforts of the two actors.

Ask the actors:

• **How did you feel when other kids harrassed you?** (Upset; angry; it didn't bother me.)

• **How is this like the way people might feel when they're picked on for their faith?** (I get upset when someone picks on me about my relationship with Christ; it doesn't bother some people.)

Then ask everyone else:

• **How did you feel supporting Diego or Señor Gonzales in this discussion?** (I liked what my character was saying; I felt more sympathy for the other character.)

• **How do you think Christians should react when they're persecuted, or when they see others being persecuted?** (They should speak out against the injustice; they should turn the other cheek.)

• **Persecution is something Christians have always faced. What motivates people to persecute Christians?** (Guilt; greed; a desire for power and control.)

Say: **Jesus warned his followers that persecution would happen, so we shouldn't be surprised when it hits. We need to learn how to respond appropriately—and we may not all respond in the same way. Let's look at some biblical responses to persecution and see how God helped the early Christians face the hardships that came to them.**

BIBLE APPLICATION

(15 to 20 minutes)

TO SPEAK OR NOT TO SPEAK?

Form two groups. Give groups each a sheet of paper and a pencil and enough Bibles for every two or three students to have one. Assign one group Acts 4:1-21 and the other group Acts 12:1-16.

Write the words "who," "why," "what" and "how" on a chalkboard or newsprint. Say: **Read through your scripture passage to discover *who* was being persecuted, *why* they were being persecuted, *what* kind of persecution it was, *how* they responded and *how* God responded.**

Give groups about five minutes to study and discuss the questions. Then bring everyone together and have groups report their findings. After both groups have reported, ask:

• **If you had been in Peter's place facing the Sanhedrin, knowing that these were some of the same men who sentenced Jesus to death about 10 years earlier, how do you think you would have responded?** (I would have kept my mouth shut; I would have responded the same way Peter did.)

• **Does everyone need to respond as Peter did? Explain.** (No— the Holy Spirit gave Peter the words to say; John was also there, but he was quiet.)

• **What can we learn from these passages that will help**

us face persecution in our lives? (God will help us know what to say; prayer works; God is capable of intervening for us.)

Say: **There is no one formula for responding to persecution. We're individuals, and God helps us and leads us in unique ways. Some are meant to be like Peter and speak out. Others are more like John—quiet, but firm in their own stand. The important thing to remember is that we don't have to face persecution alone. God will be with us, just as he was with the early Christians.**

COMMITMENT
(5 to 10 minutes)

COMFORT ZONE

Form pairs. Have partners tell each other about situations in their lives when they feel persecuted because of their faith, then brainstorm ways to respond to the persecution.

Distribute 1-foot lengths of ribbon.

Say: **Tie your ribbon around your partner's wrist. As you tie it, make a verbal commitment to your partner to pray for him or her at a certain time each day.**

When partners have finished, bring everyone together. Hand out nine Bibles as kids gather. Have each person with a Bible read aloud one verse from Romans 8:31-39 around the circle.

Say: **God promises that in all these things, we'll be "more than conquerors."**

Ask volunteers to tell about how God has given them comfort and help during times of persecution. Then say: **It's comforting to know that these promises aren't just words on a page. They're true. They were true back in Bible times and they're true today.**

CLOSING
(up to 5 minutes)

☐ OPTION 1: CIRCLE PRAYER

Form a tight circle. Have kids each extend their hand with the ribbon into the center of the circle and make a pile of hands.

Close with a prayer similar to this one: **Lord, you have promised that we would be more than conquerors in all the hardships we face because of our faith in you. Thank you for that wonderful promise. Help us to be faithful in praying for each other. In Jesus' name. Amen.**

☐ OPTION 2: UNBREAKABLE BOND

Tell kids you need a volunteer. Have the person who volunteers stand off to one side as the rest of the kids grasp hands to form a human knot in the center of a tight circle.

Say to the volunteer: **It's your job to pull this circle completely apart. Go for it!**

The volunteer will probably start pulling on the weakest person. Kids in the circle can shift their holds to hang onto that person more securely. Even if the volunteer succeeds in pulling one person away momentarily, there's no way he or she could pull the entire circle apart.

After a couple of minutes, have the volunteer join the circle.

Say: **Just as our hands have formed an unbreakable bond, the Bible tells us that nothing can separate us from the love of God. No persecution, no mockery, no exclusion—nothing. This bond we share as brothers and sisters in Christ is a big part of the support and help God gives us.**

Still hanging on to each other, have kids give thanks for the person facing them in the circle by finishing the sentence: "I'm glad (name of person facing them) is part of my support group because . . . "

Dismiss kids with the statement: **Go in God's strength and grace.**

If You Still Have Time . . .

Active or Passive Resistance?—Have kids form two teams for a debate based on the "Diego's Dilemma" handout (p. 27) used in the Action and Reflection section of this lesson. Have one side argue for passive resistance to oppressive, persecuting governments. Have the other side argue for active, open rebellion.

World View—Invite kids to share what they know of the persecution of Christians worldwide. In which countries are things really bad right now? In which countries are things improving? Brainstorm ways to encourage Christians in other countries who are facing hardships because of their faith.

DIEGO'S DILEMMA

Photocopy this handout and have volunteers read the parts of the father and son.

Sr. Gonzales: I'm glad you're finally home. I was getting worried.

Diego: I was at church.

Sr. Gonzales: The church isn't always a safe place to be—especially when you're with those revolutionaries.

Diego: Dad, we're not revolutionaries—we're just Christians. You and mom are Christians too!

Sr. Gonzales: Yes, but we don't work to overthrow the government.

Diego: We're working for schools and health care and DEMOCRACY!

Sr. Gonzales: This is dangerous business, Diego. You're putting my job and even our lives in jeopardy.

Diego: But, Dad, people are dying all around us. We can't just sit around and do nothing.

Sr. Gonzales: You know that I'll work for change in quiet ways from the inside. But we can't solve everyone's problems, Diego. If you keep up these activities we'll all be in trouble. It's best just to mind your own business and keep quiet like everyone else.

Diego: But people are dying without enough food and health care. How can you be content to work in a system that kills innocent people for standing up for what's right? Father Hernandez says it's our Christian responsibility to do something.

Sr. Gonzales: I know all about what Father Hernandez says. And he's going to get himself killed if he keeps it up. What will that accomplish? The church needs to stay out of politics.

Diego: But remember the words Jesus quoted from Isaiah: "[He] has anointed me to preach good news to the poor. He has sent me to . . . proclaim release from darkness for the prisoners, to proclaim the year of the Lord's favor."

Sr. Gonzales: I know, son. And we do what we can. But we must be patient and let God work.

Diego: Be patient? Innocent people are dying!

Sr. Gonzales: People die. It's part of being human. But we don't have to die. We can keep on living and working for change.

Diego: I guess we each have to live out our faith in our own way. My death means something if it helps save the lives of hundreds of others.

Sr. Gonzales: You're young and idealistic. I'd like to see you live to be old and idealistic.

Diego: Last night I read Paul's words: "For to me, to live is Christ and to die is gain." That's how I feel. I'm not willing to be a silent Christian.

Permission to photocopy this handout granted for local church use. Copyright © Group Publishing, Inc., Box 481, Loveland, CO 80539.

LESSON 3

TAKING THE CHURCH ON THE ROAD

It can be difficult for teenagers to see the church as something that is alive and active beyond the walls of the familiar steeple and stained-glass windows. Yet when kids see the church in terms of discipleship and evangelism, it suddenly becomes exciting and challenging. As kids discover the active church, they discover the creativity of the Holy Spirit in using people to spread God's word.

LESSON AIM

To help senior highers discover the importance of telling others about their faith.

OBJECTIVES

Students will:

- **explore how the early Christians spread God's message;**
- **struggle with the challenge of conveying the gospel message;**
- **discuss various ways to tell others about their faith; and**
- **commit to share their faith through words and actions.**

BIBLE BASIS

ACTS 8:26-40
EPHESIANS 4:11-13

Look up the following scriptures. Then read the background paragraphs to see how the passages relate to your senior highers.

In **Acts 8:26-40**, Philip is led by the spirit to share God's love with a eunuch.

While sharing faith is not always easy, this story is a great example of how the spirit prepares people's hearts to hear God's word. For just as Philip is able to share his faith with the eunuch, we too can share our faith with those around us.

Teenagers don't always feel comfortable sharing their faith. But they can be assured that the Holy Spirit will be with them as they do the work of the church in spreading God's word.

In **Ephesians 4:11-13**, Paul describes a variety of gifts that Christians have.

Paul doesn't stop at describing the various gifts Christians have but reminds us we should use our gifts to the edification of the whole community.

Teenagers can recognize the many different gifts they have. And, as Paul taught, they can encourage each other to practice those gifts to the glory of God.

THIS LESSON AT A GLANCE

Section	Minutes	What Students Will Do	Supplies
Opener (Option 1)	5 to 10	**The Heart of the Matter**—Brainstorm and share what they know about the Christian faith.	Paper, pencils
(Option 2)		**Good News**—Play a game and tell good things that happened during the previous week.	Paper plates, markers
Action and Reflection	10 to 15	**It Isn't Easy**—Discover the difficulties of telling others about their faith.	"Mixed Messages" handouts (p. 35)
Bible Application	10 to 15	**How Are We Doing?**—Explore how early Christians approached the issue of telling others about Jesus' love.	Paper, pencils, Bibles
Commitment	10 to 15	**What Can I Give?**—Think of ways to share God's love with others in word and action.	Bible
Closing (Option 1)	up to 5	**Thanks for Strength**—Thank God for giving the strength to do the work of the church.	
(Option 2)		**Reaching Out Together**—Pray for wisdom and confidence to reach out to people in need.	

The Lesson

OPENER
(5 to 10 minutes)

☐ OPTION 1: THE HEART OF THE MATTER

Give kids each a sheet of paper and a pencil. Say: **You have one minute to write on your paper everything you know about the Christian faith. Imagine you're writing this to give to someone who knows little or nothing about Christianity. Include things you think are most important. If you want, use pictures to tell what you know.**

After one minute, have kids form pairs. Have partners exchange papers and read them silently. Then have partners answer the following question:

- **What would your impression of the Christian faith be if you only knew what is written on your partner's paper?**

Allow time for answers, then say "switch," and have kids move to find new partners (while still holding their partner's paper). Have partners switch papers again, read them and answer the above question once more. Do this two or three more times. Then call time and form a circle.

Ask:

- **How did you feel as your words of wisdom were passed around to different people?** (Embarrassed; nervous; comfortable.)
- **How is that like the way we may feel when we approach others to talk about our faith? Explain.** (It's similar, I feel nervous; it's different, I don't worry about how others will feel.)

Say: **In this activity, you may have discovered a lot about the Christian faith as you read each person's paper. You shared a lot of personal information in a risky way. Today we'll explore how the church prompts us to take what we know and share it with others.**

☐ OPTION 2: GOOD NEWS

Place the same number of paper plates as you have students on the floor of your meeting room. Number them sequentially. Have kids each stand on a paper plate.

Then say: **You're going to play a simple game to see what great things have happened in your lives during the past week. When I say "wander" you can move around the room and talk among yourselves about anything you'd like. But when I say "jump!" move quickly to the nearest paper plate and stand on it. Then I'll call out a random number from one to <u>(the highest number on the plates)</u>.**

That person must quickly tell one great thing that happened this past week and why everyone should have this happen to him or her. For example: If I told about

getting an "A" on a test, I might say that everyone should get an "A" because it feels good to be smart.

Ready, wander.

Call "jump!" and a random number four or five times (or more if time allows). Then call time and have kids bring their plates and form a circle. Collect the paper plates.

Ask:

- **How did you feel when I called your number?** (Nervous; unsure; excited; worried.)
- **How is that like the way people feel when put on the spot about their faith?** (They feel nervous; they're unsure.)

Say: **One of our roles as the body of Christ is to reach out to others and tell them about our faith. Similarly, we're to help other Christians grow in their faith. Today we'll explore what it means to reach out to others and help them grow closer to God.**

ACTION AND REFLECTION

(10 to 15 minutes)

IT ISN'T EASY

Say: **We have a role in the mission of the church to bring the good news of God's love to all people. Paul traveled great distances to do this. And we also need to be ready to share our faith whenever an opportunity arises. But there are many obstacles to our work as Christians.**

Have kids form groups of no more than four. Give one person in each group a "Mixed Messages" handout (p. 35).

Say: **People holding the handouts are to let the rest of their group members know about Christ's love by reading this message aloud. Group members may ask questions, but readers may not say any other words than those on the handout. Ready, go!**

After a couple minutes, call time and ask:

- **Was it easy to understand what the readers were saying? Why or why not?** (No, it didn't make sense.)
- **How is this like the way non-Christians might hear our message if we don't use words they understand?** (They might feel frustrated; they wouldn't understand.)

Assign roles to group members. In each group, have one person be the "speaker," one be the "ignorer," one be the "denyer" and one be the "listener." Say: **Speakers, your job is to tell the others in your group about God's love for them. Ignorers, your job is to completely ignore the speaker and be obnoxious about it. Denyers, your job is to counter everything the speaker says and challenge or question it. And Listeners, your job is to listen carefully, as if you're hearing this news for the first time and are intrigued by it.**

On "go," have kids each begin their assigned role. After about three minutes, call time.

Ask the speaker:

- **How did you feel trying to get the message to the people in your group?** (Frustrated; embarrassed; nervous.)
- **How did the different people in your group make you**

feel about what you were saying? (The ignorer made me feel unimportant; the denyer irritated me; the listener made me feel welcome.)

● **How are these responses like or unlike the responses Christians get in real life when they talk about their faith? Explain.** (They're similar, many people ignore you; they're different, many people don't respond that way.)

● **What does this activity show us about the job Christians have in telling others about God's love?** (It isn't easy; Christians need to know what they're talking about; people won't always listen.)

Say: **Reaching out to others is often the most difficult role we have as Christians. That's because many people don't want to hear what we have to say.**

BIBLE APPLICATION
(10 to 15 minutes)

HOW ARE WE DOING?

Form groups of no more than five. Give groups each a sheet of paper, a pencil and a Bible. Assign each group one of the following passages: Acts 8:26-40 (Philip and the eunuch); Acts 13:16-39 (Paul in Antioch); or Acts 17:16-32 (Paul in Athens). It's okay for more than one group to have the same scripture passage.

Say: **In your group, create a simple skit to show the method or methods used by the main character (Paul or Philip) to tell others about God's love. First, read your passage and discuss what you think the methods are. Then plan your brief skit. The skit can be similar to the Bible passage or can be set in modern times.**

Allow six or seven minutes for groups to plan their skits. Then have groups each perform their skit.

After all the skits have been performed, ask:

● **How did Paul and Philip do the work of the church in these passages?** (They reached out to other people; they helped other people discover God's great love.)

● **What did these skits tell us about the way Paul and Philip told others about God's love and Jesus' sacrifice?** (Paul began by explaining what the people already knew; Paul appealed to the people's needs; Philip helped a person understand scripture.)

● **What can we learn from these examples that helps us know how to tell others about God's love?** (We can meet people where they are; we can help people understand what they don't know about God.)

● **How was the message in each of these situations similar?** (All told about Jesus' sacrifice; all told about God's love.)

Say: **Paul and Philip not only spoke, but acted on what they said. We too are called as Christians to show our love for God with our actions as well as our words.**

WHAT CAN I GIVE?

Say: **Though the whole of our lives should be a witness to God's love, we can do specific things to show our love for God.**

Form trios and have kids take turns saying one thing they can do to show God's love to others. For example, students might say visit shut-ins, take food to people who have little, help a friend with homework or spend time with people who are in the hospital. Then have trios each tell the whole group the three things they thought of.

Ask students each to choose one idea from the brainstorm and plan to follow through on it during the coming week. Have trio members commit to checking in with each other during the week to see how they're doing on their commitments.

Then ask:

- **What things about the Christian faith can be communicated without words?** (Love for others; concern; care.)

Have kids move around the room and, without words, show God's love to other people. Remind kids to be sincere and encourage them to show God's love to as many people as possible.

Then form a circle and ask:

- **How did you feel giving and receiving God's love through other class members?** (I felt happy; I felt uncomfortable.)
- **How is this like what we should be doing as members of God's church?** (We need to share God's love; we need to show how much we care for other people.)

Have a volunteer read aloud Ephesians 4:11-13, then describe a gift the person on his or her left has that will enable that person to share God's love with others. For example: A student might say, "Tom's patience will help him deal with times when people don't want to listen to what he says about God." Go around the circle until everyone has said something positive about the person on his or her left.

COMMITMENT

(10 to 15 minutes)

☐ OPTION 1: THANKS FOR STRENGTH

If possible, adjourn to the sanctuary for a time of silent prayer at the altar. Encourage kids to thank God for the strength and the challenge to do the work of the church in reaching out to others.

Have kids form a circle and put their arms around each other to close the lesson in a group hug, symbolizing the supportive nature of the church in action.

☐ OPTION 2: REACHING OUT TOGETHER

Form a circle. Ask volunteers to pray, asking God for the wisdom and confidence to reach out to people in need. As each person finishes praying, have the group say in unison, "We are the church—help us reach out together."

CLOSING

(up to 5 minutes)

If You Still Have Time . . .

Without a Word—Drawing on personal experiences and from the activities in this session, ask students to name ways they can give a non-verbal witness to their faith through actions and symbols. Have volunteers tell ways their own lives have been touched through the non-verbal witnesses of others.

Give It a Try—Form pairs and have partners practice telling each other about God's love. Encourage pairs to support their partner's attempts and to give helpful advice on how to better explain the importance of their faith. Then have volunteers tell the whole group their feelings about this exercise and what they learned.

Mixed Messages

I'm here to tell you about Jesus. You know, the one who was crucified and rose from the dead? Through him we can have forgiveness and peace with God.

But males need to wear high-top sneakers and never drink carbonated beverages. Women must grow their hair long and never listen to pop music. A man should never speak unless first spoken to by a woman.

Since women were at the foot of the cross and the first to come to Jesus' empty tomb, only women can be priests or pastors.

Places of worship must have at least six colored glass windows and an organ to make them sound like roller skating rinks.

When you do these things, you will show that your commitment to Jesus is real. And Jesus will give you the power to make half-court shots in basketball, and your hair will always have body. If you don't do these things, God won't listen to your prayers.

Permission to photocopy this handout granted for local church use. Copyright © Group Publishing, Inc., Box 481, Loveland, CO 80539.

LESSON 4

ON A MISSION

The church doesn't exist on Earth just to kill time. When Jesus ascended, he gave us a mission: To let the world know about him. In our churches and in our lives, God wants us to be working toward the fulfillment of that mission.

Help your kids understand that we do have a mission from God as Christians. It's not just a mission for the Billy Grahams or the pastors of the world. It's for all of us. Kids can learn that they too can be a part of accomplishing God's mission for the church here on Earth.

LESSON AIM

To help senior highers discover the mission God gave the church and how they can help fulfill it.

OBJECTIVES

Students will:

- **discuss what it means to have a mission;**
- **examine Bible passages related to the mission God gave the church;**
- **play a game to demonstrate different ways of fulfilling a mission; and**
- **commit to doing more to help accomplish the church's mission.**

BIBLE BASIS

ACTS 1:6-8
ACTS 10:34-43
ACTS 14:21-23

Look up the following scriptures. Then read the background paragraphs to see how the passages relate to your senior highers.

In **Acts 1:6-8**, Jesus gives his disciples a mission.

Just before Jesus departed from Earth to ascend to heaven, he told his disciples what they were to do after the Holy Spirit came to them. Their mission: To spread the news about Jesus all over the world.

As senior highers begin to decide what they're going to do with their lives, they need to keep in mind how their gifts and abilities might be used to help accomplish the mission God has given us. Whether they become doctors, factory workers, missionaries or presidents, God can use them to help spread the good news.

Acts 10:34-43 explains the message disciples of Jesus can take to the world.

It was new to Peter that God would accept people other than Jews. In his mind, the Christian God was purely the God of Abraham. God definitely is that, but he's much more. He's the God that sent his son to live among humans, to die for our sins and to rise again. Through him, and him only, can people's sins be forgiven. What an important and exciting message we have to share with our neighbors and with the world!

Acts 14:21-23 gives us a glimpse of the workings of the early church. Here we see Paul and Barnabas preaching the good news, strengthening and encouraging the disciples, and with prayer and fasting, appointing elders for the young church.

There are many aspects to the mission God has given us as Christians. We must understand what's at the center of this mission and be willing to share our talents in a variety of ways.

THIS LESSON AT A GLANCE

Section	Minutes	What Students Will Do	Supplies
Opener (Option 1)	5 to 10	**Mission Definable**—Write missions of various organizations.	Chalkboard and chalk, or newsprint and markers
(Option 2)		**Mission Possible**—Go on a simple mission and discuss different kinds of missions.	
Action and Reflection	10 to 15	**Mission Accomplished**—Play a game in which teams accomplish the same mission in different ways.	3×5 cards, 4 newspapers, 4 packs of gum, 4 pliers
Bible Application	15 to 20	**Different Missions**—Form groups and examine the church's mission.	Paper, pencils, Bibles
Commitment	5 to 10	**Our Mission**—Examine how they're helping fulfill the church's mission.	"Whose Mission Is It?" handouts (p. 42), pencils
Closing (Option 1)	up to 5	**Be Glorified**—Sing a song of commitment to serving God.	Songbooks and accompaniment
(Option 2)		**Help From Above**—Pray for God's help in fulfilling the mission he's given us.	Bible

The Lesson

OPENER
(5 to 10 minutes)

☐ OPTION 1: MISSION DEFINABLE

On a chalkboard or newsprint, draw a large outline of a football, a pop bottle, a school building and a military tank. Without giving kids time to answer, ask the following questions:

- **What's the mission of a football team?**
- **What's the mission of The Coca-Cola Company?**
- **What's the mission of your school?**
- **What's the mission of our country's armed forces?**

Then say: **Each of these drawings relates to one of the questions I just asked. Come up and write an answer to at least two of the questions inside the drawings related to those two questions.**

Give kids chalk or markers and have them write their answers. Repeat the questions if necessary. When kids are finished, have them read their answers. Then ask:

- **What's a "mission"?** (Something someone sets out to do; a goal; an assignment.)
- **What's our mission as Christians?** (To tell others about our faith in Jesus; to live the way God wants us to.)

Say: **Jesus gave the church a mission while he was here on Earth. Let's take a look at what that mission is.**

☐ OPTION 2: MISSION POSSIBLE

Before class, decide on three simple "missions" to send kids on such as collecting a signature from someone outside of class, finding a small stone, or singing a song outside the building.

When kids arrive, form three groups and give each group one of the missions you've chosen. Tell groups to be back in five minutes, then send them out on their missions.

When groups return, ask:

- **Why did you do what you just did?** (You told us to; we had a mission to accomplish.)
- **What other kinds of missions do people go on?** (Military missions; mercy missions; Christian missions.)

Say: **There are lots of different kinds of missions, but today we're going to be talking about one in particular. Jesus gave the church a mission while he was here on Earth. Let's take a look at what that mission is.**

MISSION ACCOMPLISHED

ACTION AND REFLECTION
(10 to 15 minutes)

Form four teams. A team can be one person. Assign each team one corner of the room. Place four stacks of twelve 3×5 cards in the center of the room. Designate one stack for each team. Give each team a newspaper, a pack of gum and a pair of pliers.

Say: **Your mission in this game is to get your team's cards from the center of the room out to your team's corner. But there are two catches: You may not touch any card with any part of your body, and you may not move more than one card at a time, even with all the objects you have to use. Use any or all of the objects; just be sure to follow the rules. Otherwise your team will be disqualified.**

Don't say anything about a winner or about hurrying to finish. When all teams have finished, bring the teams together and ask:

- **How did you feel when another team finished before you did? Explain.** (Lousy, I wanted to win; okay, you never said we were racing.)
- **How is this like the way you might feel when you see others doing big things to help accomplish the mission of the church?** (I get jealous because I can't do those things; I feel okay because I'm doing what God wants me to do.)
- **How was the method your team used to accomplish your mission different from the other teams' methods?**
- **Which methods worked well? Explain.**
- **Since I didn't say speed was important in this mission, which method got the mission accomplished best?** (All did the same; one team got disqualified.)
- **How is the way we used different methods in accomplishing our mission similar to the way God uses different people in his church to accomplish his mission?** (Different people have different tasks; not everybody does things the same way.)

Say: **We can all participate in accomplishing the mission God gave the church. We may not all do the same things, or do things the same way or at the same speed, but God has a way for each of us to serve him.**

DIFFERENT MISSIONS

BIBLE APPLICATION
(15 to 20 minutes)

Form groups of three or four. Give each group a sheet of paper, a pencil and a Bible. Say: **Now I'm going to give everybody a mission. We're going to examine the mission Jesus gave the church and how the early Christians began working toward fulfilling that mission. I'm going to give each group one of three different Bible passages. Your mission will be to write a paragraph defining what the early Christians saw as their mission from Christ. In your groups, look up your passages and develop your paragraphs.**

Give each group one of the following passages: Acts 1:6-8; Acts 10:34-43; Acts 14:21-23. It's okay for more than one group to have the same scripture passage.

Give groups about 10 minutes to study their passages and write their paragraphs. After 10 minutes, have groups each read their definition. Then ask:

- **How were your paragraphs similar?**
- **How were they different?**
- **Why weren't your paragraphs exactly the same?** (We all saw things differently; the people did different things in fulfilling the mission Jesus gave them.)
- **How are the differences between the paragraphs similar to the differences between Christians or churches today?** (Both are based on differences in people; both are due to different interpretations of the Bible.)
- **What was the key message of these passages?** (We're to let our world know about Jesus; we're to take action, not just sit here.)

Say: **Jesus gave us our mission as Christians. But he didn't say we were all supposed to do exactly the same thing.**

COMMITMENT
(5 to 10 minutes)

OUR MISSION

Form a circle. If you have 12 or more kids, have them return to their teams from the last activity and sit in circles. Give kids each a "Whose Mission Is It?" handout (p. 42) and a pencil. Have them discuss the first two questions as a group, then individually think about and write answers to the next two questions. Tell them not to do the last question yet.

When kids have completed the first two parts of the handout, have the whole group discuss what they wrote, going over each question and answer together. Then form pairs and have kids complete the last question on the handout. After a minute, have partners share with each other what they wrote.

Note: This might be a good time for a visit from your pastor to explain the uniqueness of your church or denomination. Be sure your pastor discusses with kids ways they can help fulfill your church's mission.

CLOSING
(up to 5 minutes)

☐ OPTION 1: BE GLORIFIED

To wrap up your session, sing together the song "Lord, Be Glorified" (*The Group Songbook*, Group Books) or some other song of commitment to serve God in his church. Close with prayer.

OPTION 2: HELP FROM ABOVE

Have a volunteer read aloud Acts 13:47. Then say: **God never gives us a mission to accomplish without giving us the ability to accomplish it. But we need to rely on him to give us what we need. Let's have a prayer time to ask God to help our church accomplish its mission in our community.**

Have kids volunteer to pray for your church, your pastor, your congregation's leaders, the people of your community and your kids themselves. Ask God to help each of you do your part in fulfilling the mission of the church.

To end your prayer time and your four-week study, read aloud Acts 13:47 again.

If You Still Have Time . . .

Me a Missionary?—Discuss how the term "missionary" ties into the word "mission." Ask:

- What does it mean to be a missionary?
- Can we be missionaries right where we are? Explain.
- What does it take to become a foreign missionary?

Encourage kids to consider if God might want them to serve him in some other part of the world.

Solid Support—Have kids brainstorm ways to support each other in their efforts to serve God. List kids' ideas as they brainstorm, then encourage kids to really help one another. You might even want to form a support group that meets regularly for encouragement.

Course Reflection—Form a circle. Ask students to reflect on the past four lessons. Have them take turns completing the following sentences:

- Something I learned in this course is . . .
- If I could tell my friends about this course, I'd say . . .
- Something I'll do differently because of this course is . . .

WHOSE MISSION IS IT?

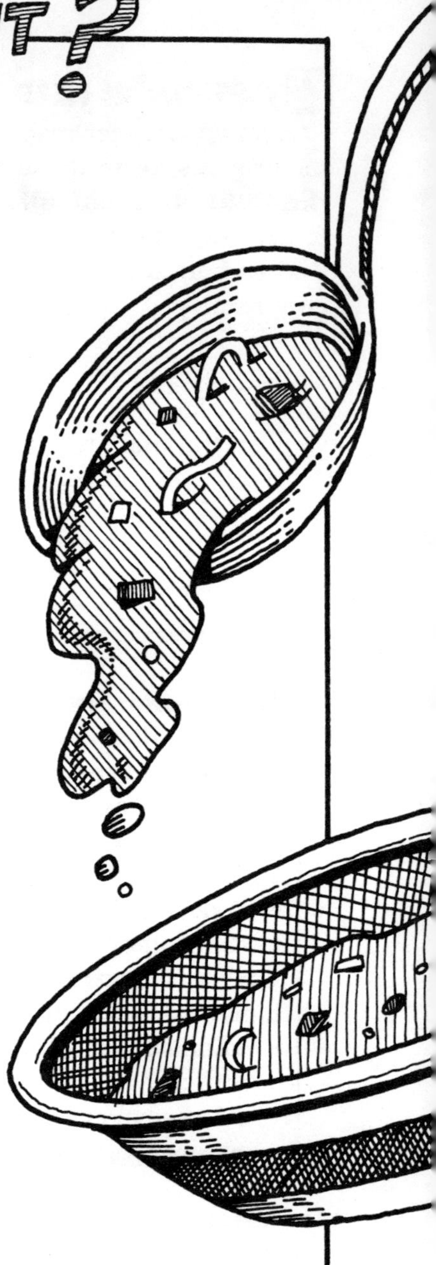

Discuss the following questions in your group:

- How is the church fulfilling its mission in the world?
- How is our church helping accomplish the church's mission?

Think about and write answers to the following questions on your own:

- How am I helping accomplish my church's mission?

- What more am I going to do to help fulfill that mission?

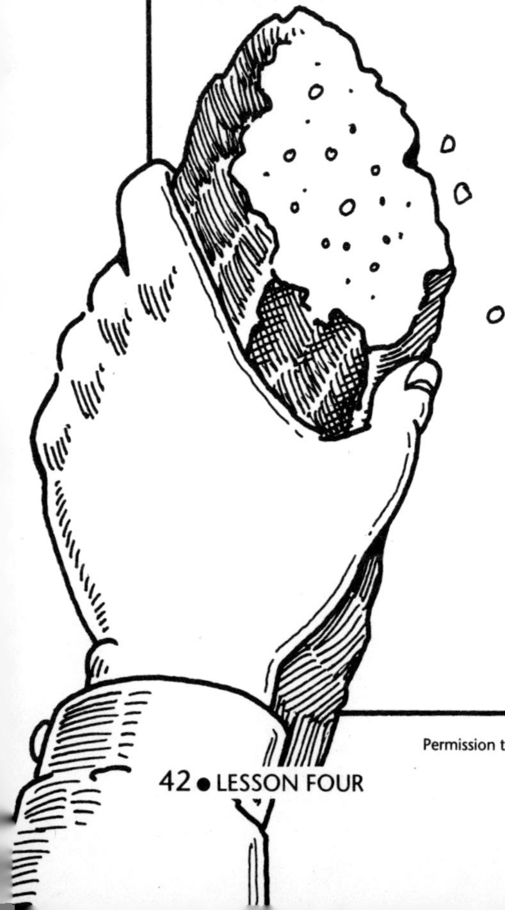

Form pairs before answering this question:

- What's one way I've seen my partner helping accomplish God's mission for the church?

Permission to photocopy this handout granted for local church use. Copyright © Group Publishing, Inc., Box 481, Loveland, CO 80539.

BONUS IDEAS

MEETINGS AND MORE

Bonus Scriptures—The lessons focus on a select few scripture passages, but if you'd like to incorporate more Bible readings into the lessons, here are our suggestions:

- Psalm 111:1 (The psalmist gives thanks to the Lord in the company of others.)
- Acts 2:41-47 (The author of Acts describes the results of Pentecost.)
- 1 Corinthians 7:17 (Paul tells Christians to do what God has called them to do.)
- Ephesians 2:19-22 (Jesus is the cornerstone of God's church.)
- 1 Thessalonians 5:12-15 (Appreciate those who work and teach.)
- 1 Timothy 3:1-13 (Paul gives instructions concerning leaders in the church.)
- Hebrews 13:17 (Obey your leaders.)

Other Traditions—Take your kids to a church with totally different traditions from your own. Encourage kids to observe the traditions and elements of the service. Have kids meet afterward with the church's pastor or priest for a brief question and answer session. Plan to debrief the entire experience once you return to your own church. See if kids discovered any good ideas you could incorporate into your church's worship service!

The Church Isn't a Building—Form groups of no more than five. Give groups each a Bible, a pencil and a copy of "The Church Isn't a Building" handout (p. 46). Have groups complete the handout and discuss it. Then have groups each tell the whole group one way they plan to be "the church" to others around them. For example: A group might say, "We plan to reach out to the needy and poor people in our community."

Spreading the Word—Invite missionaries on furlough or retired missionaries to visit your class and discuss the difficulties and challenges they face (or faced) in presenting the gospel message to people in other languages or cultures. Make arrangements ahead of time to serve snacks that represent the country the missionaries serve or served in.

Real Life Examples—Form teams of no more than four. Give teams each a Bible. Call out Bible passages from this curriculum or add your own. Teams must find the passages, then think of an example of how that particular aspect of ministry is carried out today (in your own church if applicable). The first team to send a volunteer to you gets to answer first. That team gets three points for its answer. Any other teams that answer the same question get one point each. For example: If you called out Acts 8:26-40, a team might decide your church's outreach ministry is similar to what's described in the verses and use that as their answer.

In Comparison— Ask students to write a list of specific characteristics of the Christian church including activities, decorations, forms of worship, things they find baffling, things they find strange and things they find familiar. Then have groups discuss reasons for keeping, changing or dropping these characteristics based on the mission of the church. It might be handy to have a pastor on hand to discuss the origin of some of the items discussed. Keep this from being a "what's-wrong-with-the-church" session by reminding kids they're also to explore the value of the traditions and characteristics.

Table Talk— Use the Table Talk handout (p. 19) as the basis for a meeting with parents and teenagers. During the meeting, have parents and kids complete the handout and discuss it. Then have parents and kids discuss the issues of the church's mission (in general, and specifically relating to your church).

Have parents and kids brainstorm ways they, as families, can help the church fulfill its mission.

PARTY PLEASER

Church History Comes to Life— Help teenagers plan a party where they represent famous people in church history. There are many characters to choose from, such as John the Baptist, Paul, Timothy, members of the Spanish Inquisition, Martin Luther and others. Encourage students to explore church history a bit before choosing their characters. During the party, have kids each tell about their character and his or her contribution (good or bad) to the development of the church.

Plan to serve a variety of foods representing various locations and times in church history including Greek food and German food.

RETREAT IDEAS

"The Church in Action" Retreat— Plan a retreat where you and your kids spend most of your retreat time working in a local soup kitchen, shelter or other place where people's needs are met. For added impact, have students and their parents attend and participate together.

There are many social-agency and church-sponsored programs in need of volunteers to lend a hand. Plan time at the end of the retreat to worship and eat together with the people you've been serving. Then spend a couple hours debriefing the experience and brainstorming other ways your class can translate faith into action.

Faith in the Midst of Trials—To further explore the meaning of persecution, have kids role-play being a group of Christians in a country where Christianity is against the law. Before the experience, remind kids this is just a simulation.

Begin the mini-retreat by taking your kids to a secluded area and then walking a short distance to a pre-chosen cramped meeting room (in the country, if possible). For an added sense of realism, have "soldiers" patrol the area near where you meet, so that it's necessary for kids to sneak past them to get to the meeting place. To make even more of an impact, have the soldiers "capture" one or two "Christians" as they attempt to get to the meeting room (you'll have to arrange this with the soldiers and those people ahead of time).

During your meeting, have volunteers tell what Christ has been doing in their lives. Read scriptures and talk about how you can share God's love even if others mock or ridicule you.

Afterward, have the whole group meet in familiar surroundings to discuss their feelings during this experience. Discuss questions such as:

- How is the way you felt in this experience like or unlike how you feel at school or home each day?
- How was today's "persecution" different from that experienced by Christians of the early church?
- How can we overcome persecution and live boldly for Christ?

THE CHURCH ISN'T A BUILDING

Although "going to church" usually means heading for a building with a steeple, stained glass windows and a pulpit, the church Jesus set up on Earth isn't a building at all. *We* are the church.

Read the following scripture passages and talk about ways your group can be the church in your community. List each idea on one section of the church building below.

Read:
- Leviticus 19:34
- Luke 14:27-35
- John 13:34
- Acts 20:28
- 1 Corinthians 12:5
- Colossians 3:11

Permission to photocopy this handout granted for local church use.
Copyright © Group Publishing, Inc., Box 481, Loveland, CO 80539.

CURRICULUM REORDER—TOP PRIORITY

Order now to prepare for your upcoming Sunday school classes, youth ministry meetings and weekend retreats! Each book includes all teacher and student materials—plus photocopiable handouts—for any size class.

FOR SENIOR HIGH:

Quantity

_______ **Christians in a Non-Christian World**
ISBN 1-55945-224-2

_______ **Counterfeit Religions**
ISBN 1-55945-207-2

_______ **Dating Decisions**
ISBN 1-55945-215-3

_______ **Exodus: Following God**
ISBN 1-55945-226-9

_______ **Exploring Ethical Issues**
ISBN 1-55945-225-0

_______ **Faith for Tough Times**
ISBN 1-55945-216-1

_______ **Forgiveness**
ISBN 1-55945-223-4

_______ **Getting Along With Parents**
ISBN 1-55945-202-1

_______ **The Gospel of John: Jesus' Teachings**
ISBN 1-55945-208-0

_______ **Hazardous to Your Health: AIDS, Steroids & Eating Disorders**
ISBN 1-55945-200-5

_______ **Is Marriage in Your Future?**
ISBN 1-55945-203-X

_______ **Jesus' Death & Resurrection**
ISBN 1-55945-211-0

_______ **The Joy of Serving**
ISBN 1-55945-210-2

Quantity

_______ **Knowing God's Will**
ISBN 1-55945-205-6

_______ **Life After High School**
ISBN 1-55945-220-X

_______ **Making Good Decisions**
ISBN 1-55945-209-9

_______ **Money: A Christian Perspective**
ISBN 1-55945-212-9

_______ **Movies, Music, TV & Me**
ISBN 1-55945-213-7

_______ **Overcoming Insecurities**
ISBN 1-55945-221-8

_______ **Responding to Injustice**
ISBN 1-55945-214-5

_______ **School Struggles**
ISBN 1-55945-201-3

_______ **Sex: A Christian Perspective**
ISBN 1-55945-206-4

_______ **What Is the Church?**
ISBN 1-55945-222-6

_______ **Who Is God?**
ISBN 1-55945-218-8

_______ **Who Is Jesus?**
ISBN 1-55945-219-6

_______ **Who Is the Holy Spirit?**
ISBN 1-55945-217-X

_______ **Your Life as a Disciple**
ISBN 1-55945-204-8

FOR JUNIOR HIGH/MIDDLE SCHOOL:

Quantity

_______ **Accepting Others: Beyond Barriers & Stereotypes**
ISBN 1-55945-126-2

_______ **Applying the Bible to Life**
ISBN 1-55945-116-5

_______ **Becoming Responsible**
ISBN 1-55945-109-2

_______ **Boosting Self-Esteem**
ISBN 1-55945-100-9

_______ **Caring for God's Creation**
ISBN 1-55945-121-1

_______ **Christmas: A Fresh Look**
ISBN 1-55945-124-6

_______ **Dealing With Death**
ISBN 1-55945-112-2

_______ **Drugs & Drinking**
ISBN 1-55945-118-1

_______ **Evil and the Occult**
ISBN 1-55945-102-5

_______ **Genesis: The Beginnings**
ISBN 1-55945-111-4

_______ **Guys & Girls: Understanding Each Other**
ISBN 1-55945-110-6

_______ **Handling Conflict**
ISBN 1-55945-125-4

_______ **Heaven & Hell**
ISBN 1-55945-131-9

Quantity

_______ **Is God Unfair?**
ISBN 1-55945-108-4

_______ **Love or Infatuation?**
ISBN 1-55945-128-9

_______ **Making Parents Proud**
ISBN 1-55945-107-6

_______ **Making the Most of School**
ISBN 1-55945-113-0

_______ **Materialism**
ISBN 1-55945-130-0

_______ **Miracles!**
ISBN 1-55945-117-3

_______ **Peace & War**
ISBN 1-55945-123-8

_______ **Peer Pressure**
ISBN 1-55945-103-3

_______ **Prayer**
ISBN 1-55945-104-1

_______ **Sermon on the Mount**
ISBN 1-55945-129-7

_______ **Telling Your Friends About Christ**
ISBN 1-55945-114-9

_______ **The Ten Commandments**
ISBN 1-55945-127-0

_______ **Today's Music: Good or Bad?**
ISBN 1-55945-101-7

_______ **What's a Christian?**
ISBN 1-55945-105-X

Order today from your favorite bookstore, or write: Group Publishing, Box 485, Loveland, CO 80539. For mail orders, please add postage/handling of $3 for orders up to $15, $4 for orders of $15.01+. Colorado residents add 3% sales tax.

NOW YOU CAN TEACH ACTIVE BIBLE LESSONS TO 5TH- AND 6TH-GRADERS . . .

. . . with Group's NEW **Hands-On Bible Curriculum™**

Make learning fun and watch your kids' enthusiasm for the Bible grow!

Group's new **Hands-On Bible Curriculum™** will help you teach the Bible in a whole new way. Your 5th- and 6th-graders will pay attention to your lesson. They'll be more eager to learn. You'll teach lessons your kids understand and really apply to their daily lives—because Group's **Hands-On Bible Curriculum™** uses lively active learning experiences, not passive lecture, to bring home the Bible truth.

In each session, your students will participate in a variety of fun and memorable learning experiences using discovery tools you've not seen with any other curriculum. These fascinating gadgets and gizmos help your 5th- and 6th-graders discover biblical truths and remember what they learn—because they're doing instead of just listening.

Save yourself time and money with these complete discovery-packed kits!

While your students are learning more, you'll be working less—simply following the quick and easy instructions in the Teachers Guide. Lesson-planning is a cinch with Group's **Hands-On Bible Curriculum™**. You'll get plenty of material for a fast-paced 35- to 60-minute session. And, if you still have time, there's an arsenal of Bonus Ideas and Time Stuffers to keep kids occupied—and learning!

In addition to the easy-to-use Teachers Guide, you'll get all the essential teaching materials you need in a ready-to-use kit called the **Learning Lab™**. No more running from store to store hunting for lesson materials—all the active-learning tools you need are included in the **Learning Lab™**. You'll get everything you need to teach 13 exciting Bible lessons to any size class! Plus, you'll SAVE BIG over other curriculum programs that require you to buy expensive separate student books—all student handouts may be photocopied from the included masters.

Capture your kids' attention with 3 interesting topics every 13 weeks!

Group's **Hands-On Bible Curriculum™** covers topics that support the needs of your young people—as well as your church's need to teach the Bible with integrity. Every quarter you'll explore 3 meaningful subjects. One is centered around learning about others . . . another helps your students learn about themselves . . . and a third teaches your kids about God. Switching topics every month keeps your 5th- and 6th-graders enthused and coming back for more. The full 2-year program will help your kids . . .

- make God-pleasing lifestyle choices
- appreciate their God-given potential
- seek to grow as Christians
- ask for God's help in daily decisions

Take the boredom out of Sunday school, children's church, mid-week meetings and youth group for your 5th- and 6th-graders . . . and make your teachers' jobs easier and more rewarding . . . with no-fail lessons that are ready in a flash! Order Group's **Hands-On Bible Curriculum™** for your 5th- and 6th-graders today.

Group's **Hands-On Bible Curriculum™**, Quarter 1

Friendships
Self-Esteem
God's Love

Teachers Guide **ISBN 1-55945-300-1 $14.95**
Learning Lab™ **ISBN 1-55945-301-X $34.95**

Order today from your favorite bookstore, or write: Group Publishing, Box 485, Loveland, CO 80539. For mail orders, please add postage/handling of $3 for orders up to $15, $4 for orders of $15.01+. Colorado residents add 3% sales tax.